3/06

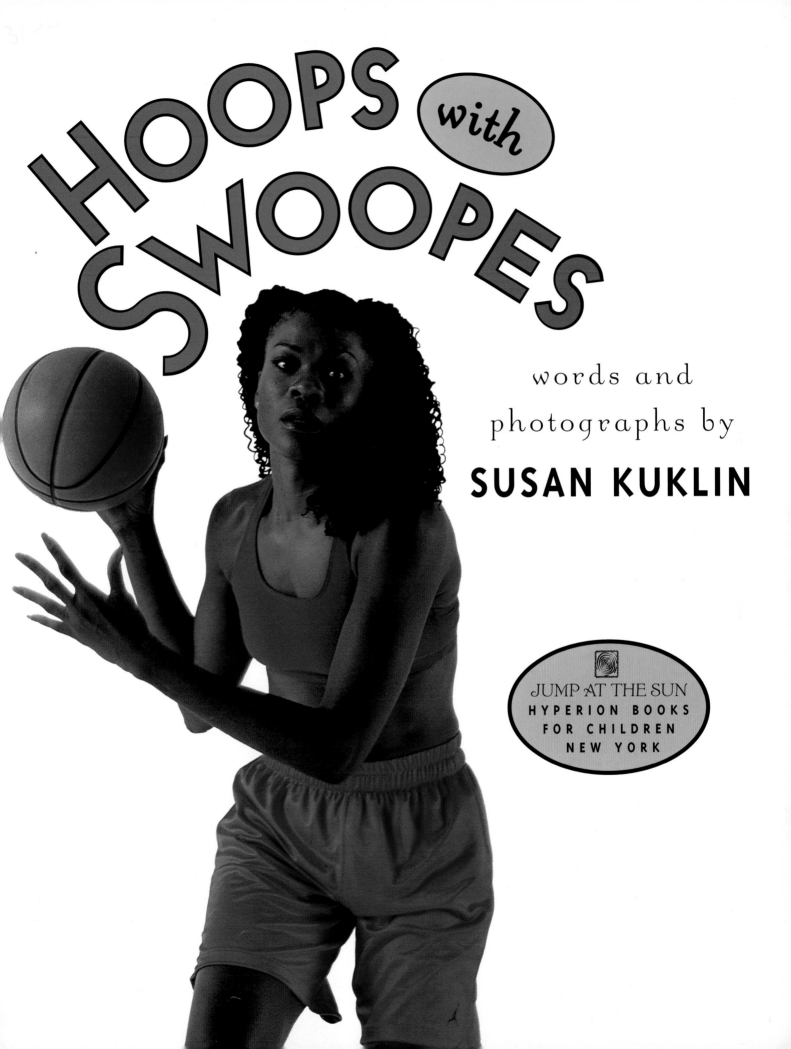

Hoops with Swoopes

words and
photographs by
SUSAN KUKLIN

JUMP AT THE SUN
**HYPERION BOOKS
FOR CHILDREN
NEW YORK**

The fundamentals are a very important part of the game. I do a lot of individual work on the fundamentals. It shows me my strengths and my weaknesses. I'm never satisfied with just winning. I can always improve something. I can become a better player—I can become a better person.

This takes practice.

But the most important thing of all is to enjoy what you do and believe in yourself. As long as you believe in yourself, anything is possible.
—Sheryl Swoopes

For Leni Sarah, and for all the girls and boys who run—jump—score!
—S.K.

Text copyright © 2001 by Susan Kuklin

Photographs copyright © 2001 by Susan Kuklin

For information address

Hyperion Books for Children, 114 Fifth Avenue, New York, New York 10011-5690.

First Edition

1 3 5 7 9 10 8 6 4 2

Printed in Hong Kong

Book design by Susan Kuklin and Christine Kettner

Library of Congress Cataloging-in-Publication Data

Kuklin, Susan.

Hoops with Swoopes / Susan Kuklin.

p. cm.

ISBN 0-7868-0551-X (trade)

1. Basketball—Juvenile literature.

[1. Swoopes, Sheryl. 2. Basketball players.

3. Women—Biography. 4. Afro-Americans—Biography.] I. Title.

GV885.1 .K85 2001   796.323—dc21

00-63887

Visit www.jumpatthesun.com

Sheryl Swoopes
shoots hoops.

CATCH

JUMP

SHOOT

STEP

She plays basketball.

DEFEND!

dribbledribbledribble

She plays from
RIGHT to LEFT—

dribbledribble

from the tips of
her fingers—

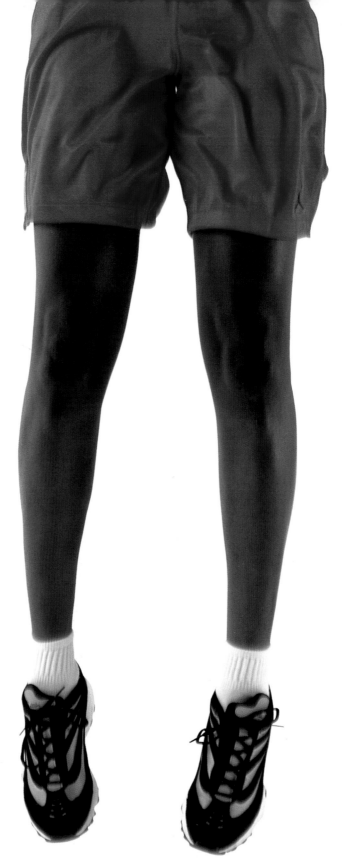

to the tips of her toes.

Her game is
concentration.

Sheryl Swoopes
shoots hoops.

SCORE

BOUNCE

Her game is
p a s s i n g —

and catching—
and
driving
down
the court.

STOP!

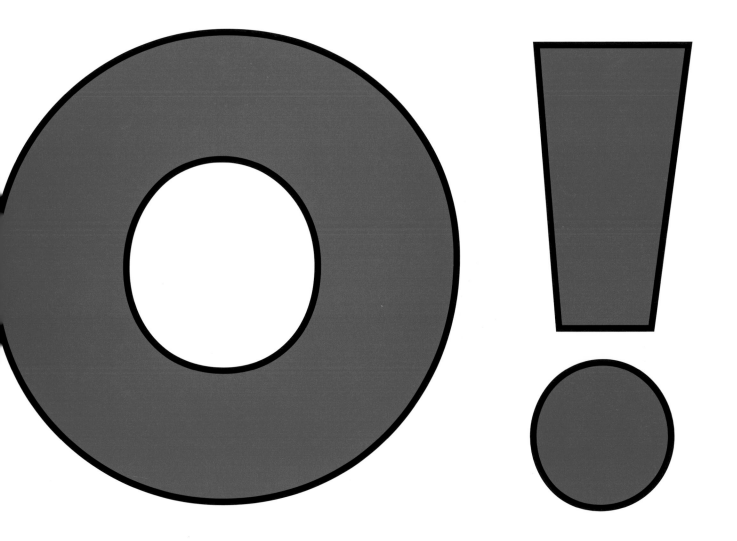

Sheryl Swoopes plays basketball

FAKE

down on the ground

up in the
A I R

REBOUND

in your
FACE

everywhere!

RUN

Her game is believing

BLOCK

CATCH

in the team—

and in herself.

Sheryl Swoopes
shoots
hoops!